# REALITY POEMS

# REALITY POEMS

Vera Gregory

Sunesis Ministries Ltd

Reality Poems

Copyright © 2016 Vera Gregory. The right of Vera Gregory to be identified as author of this work has been asserted by her in accordance with the Copyright, Designs, and Patents Act 1988. All rights reserved. No part of this publication may be reproduced or transmitted in any form or by any means, electronic or mechanical, including photocopy, recording, or any information storage and retrieval system, without permission in writing from the author.

ISBN 978-0-9935147-9-1

Published by Sunesis Ministries Ltd. For more information about Sunesis Ministries Ltd, please visit:

www.stuartpattico.com

The views expressed in this book are solely those of the author and do not necessarily reflect the views of the publisher, and the publisher hereby disclaims any responsibility for them. The author accepts sole legal responsibility for the contents of this book.

Vera Gregory was born in Jamaica. She had Elementary and Secondary Education in Jamaica.
The college in the UK Migrated at age 20
Here she did nurse training and enjoyed working in different areas in the nursing field.

Acknowledgement

My thanks to all those who have assisted me with this book.

**Tony**
**Angelica**
**Jemela**
**VJ**

# Contents

| | |
|---|---|
| LIFE | 15 |
| ANCIENT TRAVEL | 16 |
| THE SUN | 18 |
| THE EYES | 19 |
| TEACHER | 20 |
| WALK | 21 |
| TOM'S RESTAURANT | 22 |
| THE COACH | 23 |
| DRIVER SMITH | 24 |
| HANDS | 25 |
| Men | 26 |
| FLORAL TRIBUTES | 28 |
| THE PEOPLE'S ROSE | 29 |
| SPIRITS | 30 |
| RELATIONSHIP | 31 |
| THE HIGH-FLYER | 32 |
| PAIN | 33 |
| THE HEARING ORGAN | 34 |
| WOMEN | 35 |
| THE MOBILE PHONE | 36 |

SUGAR ............................................................................. 37

LIFE JOURNEY ................................................................ 38

LOVE IS IN THE AIR ....................................................... 39

WHAT AM I? .................................................................... 40

THE BIRDS ...................................................................... 42

GRANDKIDS .................................................................... 44

SUNDAY SCHOOL ......................................................... 46

PEOPLE ........................................................................... 47

BODY LANGUAGE ......................................................... 48

THE BUTCHER ............................................................... 49

TRAIN .............................................................................. 50

WORK .............................................................................. 52

SAY IT WITH FLOWERS ............................................... 53

THE FASCINATING ROSE ........................................... 55

TRIBUTES TO DIANA .................................................... 56

RAIN ................................................................................. 57

ENDURANCE .................................................................. 58

THE BOX THAT SPEAKS .............................................. 59

FLOWERS ....................................................................... 61

THE MARKET POLICE .................................................. 62

MOTHER .......................................................................... 63

FRUITS ............................................................................ 64

| | |
|---|---|
| BIRTHDAY | 65 |
| TRAVEL | 66 |
| SIXTY | 67 |
| ALARM CLOCK | 68 |
| DEATH | 69 |
| A TIME | 70 |
| PAPA, MAMA | 71 |
| GRANDMA'S ROCKING CHAIR | 72 |
| GRASS | 73 |
| THE PARK | 74 |
| WASHING MACHINE | 75 |
| THE ZOO | 76 |
| THE BUS | 77 |
| MICE | 78 |
| Funfair | 80 |
| Spectacles | 81 |
| THE BEGGAR | 82 |
| The Almighty | 83 |
| Walking stick | 84 |
| Birds | 85 |
| POLICE | 86 |
| THE SEA | 87 |

| | |
|---|---|
| GOD'S CREATION | 88 |
| FEET | 89 |
| THE SUN | 90 |
| LOVE | 91 |
| LOOKING BACK | 92 |
| TEARS | 93 |
| LANGUAGE | 94 |
| MOTOR CAR | 95 |
| MUSIC | 96 |
| Soil | 97 |
| Alone | 99 |
| The cruise | 101 |
| The willow tree | 102 |
| The beef scare | 104 |
| WHAT AM I? | 106 |
| Can you guess? | 107 |
| Hygiene | 108 |
| My kitchen | 110 |
| Jermaine | 111 |
| Evening | 112 |
| I am scared of the dark | 113 |
| Market | 114 |

Money .................................................................. 115
Handsworth Park ................................................. 116
Supermarkets ...................................................... 118
Trees ................................................................... 119
Memorable Holiday ............................................. 120
Christmas ............................................................ 122
Storm .................................................................. 124
Feeling inferior ................................................... 125
Sleep ................................................................... 126
The Human pump ............................................... 127
House .................................................................. 128
Rainy day ............................................................. 130
Charity ................................................................. 131
Rubbish ............................................................... 132
West Indian carnival ........................................... 133
The squirrel ......................................................... 134
Time .................................................................... 136
Island in the sun ................................................. 136
A to Z .................................................................. 138
Dreams ................................................................ 139
Slow Love ............................................................ 140

# LIFE

A gift from the creator,
One to cherish and to care.
There are many pleasures, But
challenges are sure.
Life is not always a bed of roses.

Life is to be enjoyed and treasured.
Be it long or be it short. The maths
for life could be, Three score years
and ten.
Plus ten more,
There could be more tens.
Who knows?
Treasure the gift.
No suicide pack!

# ANCIENT TRAVEL

Originally man's movements, Were
mainly by foot.
In some countries cow and
Donkeys were saddled,
With hampers attached,
These animals relieve man,
Of travel by foot,
Then they could avoid complaining, My
foot, my foot.

As time goes by buggies,
Came into use, Then
cars came into use.
One of the oldest motor cars,
Was the ford car,
Which only the wealthy could afford.

## THE SUN

The sun, it rises at dawn.
It glitters across the skies,
And lights the earth by day,
It lifts the spirits,
And takes the gloom away.

The sun, it helps the plant to grow,
And bring forth food. It encourage
the women, To wash, more and
more.

The sun, it melts the snow.
It dries the earth.
It shines most days.
Then hides its face at eve.

# THE EYES

Those important organs,
They give us full awareness,
Of the spot, of ground, on which, We
stand to view, and chat.

Oh what an awesome wonder,
To behold God's creation, The hills,
the rocks, the mountains, The flying
birds, the trees, the valleys.
The rivers and the vast oceans.

How wonderful to behold:
The sunrise, the sunset,
The shining moon, the shooting stars.
To view the humble and stately buildings.
To view the colourful vehicles dashing.

Without sight all must seem imaginary.
Without sight there must be fears at times.
Let's be thankful for the gift of sight.

# TEACHER

Mr, Edwards, the maths teacher, Introduced
himself to the class.
Then he said, "You are here to learn all you can.
Talking is forbidden during classes. I
need your attention.
Don't be shy to ask me, If
you have any questions.

Youth is in your favour.
Work while you are young.
Try to be good listeners.
Keen interest will pay off.
Be ambitious!

Your parents will be proud.
Of your efforts and your results.
You will eventually overcome the challenges.
And achieve your goal."

# WALK

Who wants to remain in one place,
Day after day,
Not even the baby.
He tries to creep and then to walk.
If he drops on his bottom, He will
not stay down.
He will get up again.
He will try to walk like others.

I must walk from place to place.
I must not stay too long in one place.
Or else my muscles and joints, Will
eventually become seized.

A daily walk up and down the garden, Will
increase body strength.
A walk to the shop is even better, To
get the items we need to seek after.
I t is worth while leaving the car,
At home some times,
While the body gets some exercise.
A mile walk each day, Will
help along life's way.

# TOM'S RESTAURANT

A place where variety is found.
A place to bring your friends.
A place to be remembered.
So don't fast or starve!
Just read the menu!
You will find one to suit you.
Food is prepared and cooked the best.
To create cut above the rest.

Customers are made to feel pleased, When their money they released.
The staffs treat customers with respect.
Their weekly wage they must protect.
Service is given with a smile.

Comfortable seats are also provided.
For those who wish to relax, After a satisfying meal.

# THE COACH

"Miles, and miles and miles and miles.
They must add up to millions.
I don't get much break.
Very little in the winter months.
At times you board me,
To the point of breaking.
Good thing I was built strong. So
when I take you on journeys long, I
can endure and remain strong.
Half an hour break at the service station.
A break for you and I!

# DRIVER SMITH

"I have not been to the Isle of White, Before,
said, driver Smith.
So the traffic signs I must follow.
I must also consult my satnav.
For finding places, it's better than I am.
Mostly long stretching roads I would like, But
we'll see as we ride.
I would not be surprised if I have,
To cope with a few,
Unexpected winding roads. This
coach is serviced regularly, On
it we can rely.

At midday we arrived at our destination.
Many were the tourist attractions.
Gifts shops galore.
Driver Smith said, don't let your partners, Have
to track you down.
So much to purchase.
Watch your purse.
Or else,
You return,
To the coach penny less.

# HANDS

A pair of human instruments.
Our God given body member.
Often taken for granted,
What if we had no hands?
We would be grumbling.
We rely on our hands to feed our selves.
We rely on our hands to do the cleaning.
They help us to use tools,
To operate machinery.
They help us to shape,
The clay into pottery.
To set out on paper, What
our brains perceive.
Without our hands how,
Would tasks be done?

# Men

The stronger of the human race.
They have made the ships, To
sail the seas.
The aeroplane to take the skies.
The bridges to carry incredible weights.
The tunnels, what great achievements!

They have the guts to go to war!
At times fighting, to capture other lands.
They have the guts to shoot down war planes!
At times with many loss of lives, On both
sides!
Is it worth the loss?
We are dying year by year.
But the land will be still here!
Men have achieved so much on earth; Yet
they decide they must go to other planets!

## FLORAL TRIBUTES

Overwhelming were the floral tributes, To
the English Rose.

Some lay like large patchworks, Outside
Buckingham Palace.

Young Prince Williams and Harry were amazed,
As they viewed the tributes,
And watched the crowd who gathered,
Outside the palace, To
share their grief.

Fascinating carpets of floral tributes too,
Along the roads where the princess took,
Her final journey to althorn, Her final
resting place.

A sea of flowers,
Still carpeted the grounds, Of
Kensington Palace weeks after,
The nations lost their princess.

The seas of floral tributes,
Are some symbols,
Of what the nations felt,
In their hearts, For the
Queen at heart.

# THE PEOPLE'S ROSE

She will never be forgotten, Neither
by the old nor the young.
Many will remember her touches,
As she shook hands and uttered kind words.

She gave some children hope and courage, Comforted
in her arms, through sick and diseased.
In war stricken zones.
Some had no mums or dads to call their own.

The sufferers of AIDS can be touched she showed.
Usually people distant themselves, from such cases,
Afraid to shake hands or to touch;
Though this disease is mainly sexually transmitted.

She did not have to leave her Palace,
To be with the poor, the sick. And
some dying, in devastated places; But
this was the role she chose.

## SPIRITS

No longer mortal, but immortal,
Spirits, hers and his,
Will always meet in bliss uninvaded.

Together they left this world,
End of August ninety-seven, Apparently,
just hours apart.

Even some minutes before the crash,
Some moments of caress,
Unknowingly, to be the last,  This
side of life.

Out they set to love and to cherish,
But the tragedy occurred. So
abruptly, one can scarcely decide,
Whether it's true or false!

Mourn no more you nations,
Di and Dodi spirits, Will
never part!

# RELATIONSHIP

It is like a magnet always drawing,
That powder which is ever attracting,
Like links of chains ever binding,
Those strong cords with no intent to sever.

Dare anyone to disturb, The
focus is on each other.
Everything else, Must
take second place.

Then comes the moment of decision.
He pops the question.
Will you marry me?
This sets off increased heart beat.
Face flushing,
Minds as though in a trance, The
reply is usually. I will!
Or I need time to think.

Decision could occur whilst sipping champagne,
Or whilst strolling together in the breezy twilight, Or
even at dinner whilst enjoying the exotic meal, Or
whilst applying the occasional peck on the cheek.

Marriage is a gamble!
Love is blind, they say!

# THE HIGH-FLYER

I fly, I fly, from ground to way up in the sky.
I fly, I fly, not like a bee or a fly.
I fly, I fly, like an eagle soaring the sky.
I fly, I fly, so elegant am I.

I mount, I mount, over local lands.
I mount, I mount, over distant lands.
I mount, I mount, over waters shallow to see.
I mount, I mount, over waters cool and deep.

I soar, I soar, thousands and thousands of feet.
I take you where you will.
I take you young and old.
I take your luggage too.

Man's high intellect developed me.
Man's active hands have helped to shape me.
My makers found great sense of satisfaction.
For many commuters their dreams come to fruition.

Once most people were highly elated, When
they got a glimpse of me.
Nowadays, nearly everyone knows and uses me.
And I fly; I fly to where you will.

# PAIN

Thou ugly enemy!
Bugging, bugging people,
From generation to generation, Human
can do without you.

Thou has caused much agony.
Thou has caused much tears.
Your victims have lost their joy. Men
and women are left limping, Some
bent like old baboons.

Thou has attacked humans from head to toe.
"My head, my head" they complain.
Aching stomachs, feet and joints.
You have your victims limping.

Get hence, get hence.
Humans can do without you.
Go back from whence you came.
Get hence, get hence, go and be no more.

# THE HEARING ORGAN

If we had no ears how would we appreciate sounds in the air.
If we had no ears we would miss out, on some vital information!
Their instruction, their knowledge, their affection, Their sighing, their crying, their laughing.

If we had no ears how would we hear the humming birds?
If we had no ears how would we hear the clapping thunder?
If we had no ears how would we hear the whistling winds? If we had no ears how would we hear the meowing of the cats?

If we had no ears how would females hear the males wooing?
If we had no ears how would males hear the female responding?

We cannot blame our ears for what we hear, The good, the bad and the independent.

# WOMEN

Years ago women were mainly housekeepers.
Then they strive to be of worth in the workplaces.
Women doing the same work as men were paid less.
Next they struggled to be paid equally.

Women are considered the weaker vessels.
They do not intend the man to overrule.
They have a task to replenish the earth.
Most women have a closer bond with their off springs.
As fathers spend more hours doing bread winning.

Women automatically become home managers. To
cope with jobs as well as their domestic chores,
They should manage time well.
They should practice good morals. So the
children will behave well at home, As well
as when they go to Rome. Keen interest in
their children's education, Will assist their
children's concentration.

Women should be careful with the pennies, And
be watchful of the bank balances.

# THE MOBILE PHONE

A smart equipment, Now, Pocket size
and used all over the world.
As long as you know the number.
Just press some buttons,
To give your friend a buzz.
In just a few minutes you'll be chatting.

You must have sufficient credit. The
phone company will not credit today,
Then accept pay tomorrow.

Thanks to recent competition.
Even the poor can empty their piggy banks,
After following their saving plans, To
purchase a mobile phone.

To make phone calls,
People had to walk even miles originally.
Now such walk can be avoided totally.
The phone booths now stand idle.

With added services, the mobile phones, Also
provide fun as well as information.

# SUGAR

A spoonful of sugar,
Makes the medicine,  Go
down.

A child
Will easier
Take his
Medicine
When given
A sweet
Or a teaspoon Full
of sugar.

Some folks say,
"I am sweet enough, I
don't need sugar".

It's not an issue
As most foods
And drinks Contain
sugar.

Less sugar
Less tooth decay Less sugar
related diseases.

# LIFE JOURNEY

We become substance from the womb, At
the fusion of the male and female cells.
Unique lives begin.
The embryo is nourished whilst attached to mother.

Body parts begin to develop, Not
many months after conception.
What a marvellous transformation.
Despite morning sickness, And
weight consciousness.
Mothers try to cope.
And remains proud.
Fathers too feel a sense of pride.

At seven to nine months, the baby, Pops out into
the new environment. Breast or bottle fed they
must be well nourished, For healthy
development. At age one most children walk,
And are also able to talk.
Around age two,
Discipline begins in the home.
Children are copycats,
So parents must be good role models.

Teenagers are encouraged to be ambitious. Many
have their dreams fulfilled.
And enjoy the pleasant things,
This world has to offer, for many years.
The ideas which spring to mind,
Help to shape our journey to the end.

# LOVE IS IN THE AIR

With this special person Shawn wants to share,
Some precious moments and hope that she cares.
Softly he utters some enticing words, And waited
her words to hear.

The thought of caressing his dearest,
Lingers in his mind and finds rest.
Since they winked at each other last, Twilight,
the next day seemed the longest. Shawn
worked well, but was rather anxious, To hear
the work's clock struck.

On arriving home, he had the quickest shower ever,
Then, whilst rushing through the door that evening,
He said, hurriedly, "See you later mother, I shall be
eating out with Marla".

On their first evening at McDonalds restaurant, They
chatted freely, no evidence of restraint.
They discovered that their hobbies were much the same.
They enjoyed each other company as well as the meal.
Shawn didn't bother calling a taxi.
Whilst walking Marla home, he set the next date.

# WHAT AM I?

Fruity, fruity,

And quite filling.

Add me to your diet, I beg,

Breakfast, lunch or supper.

Eat me fresh,

Ripe or green.

Useful for porridge too.

Cakes and chips and dumplings too.

With time to spare,

Boil me green,

Salt to taste, Give you a

delicious breakfast.

A good start for the day.

A good source of iron.

Go eat bananas if you can.

# THE BIRDS

They are migratory creatures.
Some travel miles upon miles to other countries.
They do not need ships or aeroplanes.
Their instincts lead them to where they will.
On their wings too they must rely.

They build their nets in trees,
On the roofs of buildings too.
They build nests in which, to lay their eggs.
Sometimes they can be seen,
Bringing food to their young, in their nest.
Like humans, they too care for their young,
Until they are old enough, To fend for themselves.

Boys sometimes use their catapults,
To shoot birds down. When the
boys return, from Bird hunting.
They make wood fire,
Then roast birds on the coals.
We all had our share.
Finger licking they were.
No oil used yet our fingers were left greasy.

## GRANDKIDS

Scarcely anything can remain as it were.
My grandkids like to see things untidy. How queer?
The one year old is destructive but curious.
She copies everything the other kids do.

It is fun to see my grandkids at play! But it is
heartbreaking to see what I have to pay, Dozens
of cassette tapes all reeling!
Small pieces of furniture left with legs breaking.

They always want each other's toys, They
often scream "It's mine, It's mine".
The training of learning to share.
Does not seem to be taken in.

Wallpaper stripped, the little one thinks it is funny, When
she sees me coming, she starts running.

Glad to see the grand's come,
Once they have gone,
The clearing up has to be done,
No more ransacking until next time they come.

# SUNDAY SCHOOL

Like early childhood schools, Sunday
school helps to set the foundation, For
early education.
Children can attend from two years of age, Providing
mum and dad agree.

They are thought moral guidance, Which
will help them to behave well?
At home and elsewhere.

The children are encouraged to take part, In
singing, with actions.
It is delightful to parents,
To see their little ones,
Clapping their tiny hands, whilst singing.

A part of the Sunday school sessions, Is
set aside for sketches.
When given crayon and paper,
The children bring out their,
Imaginative ideas of the bible stories, Which
they are being taught.

Each child receives a prize, At
the end of the year.
One is for repeating,
The golden text from memory,
(A short scripture verse)
Each child receives a reward!
No one is left in tears.

# PEOPLE

They are found all over the globe.
Tall people, short people, Fat
people, thin people.
Some like giants, Some
like dwarves.

People's skin colours vary wherever we go.
Dark skinned people,
Fair skinned people,
Red or yellow,
Black or white;
All are precious in God's sight.

Some are rich, some are poor.
According to the creator, The
rich should help the poor. It
can be agreed, "the haves,
Should help, the have nots".

Some people do love their neighbours.
Some have no concern or interest in others.
What a wonderful world it would be, If
everyone loved everyone.

## BODY LANGUAGE

Body language is expressed in various ways:
Depending on what we see,
Depending on what we hear,
Depending on what we smell, Depending
on what we taste.

Depending on what the brain allows us to see,
We blink our eyes,
Avoiding irritation by dust or flies.

The shaking of the head can indicate,
Our agreement or disagreement, With
what we hear.

If the barbecue coals burn our fingers, We
would quickly withdraw them.
If the words uttered are unpleasant,
Our facial expression changes to match our feelings.
The master of body language is the brain.

# THE BUTCHER

Many stalls laid out,
As each butcher must go out,
To make his living before the day is out.

Butcher Brown in his appeal,
Says, "Lovely beef steak, Come
see for yourself".
He weighs pieces, ready for sale.
Customers choose what they like best.

Butcher Morgan shouted from his stall, "Mutton over here".
Then Butcher Parks shouted, from his stall, "Pork over here".

Some customers buy, enough to store.
Meat market only opens certain days.
Since competition is high.
Prices should be reasonable.
Even the poor should be able, To buy
what is needed, for their table.

# TRAIN

Behold she comes running along her track, Like
a gigantic snake.
She has no time to hesitate. Get
out of her way, or you will be,
Like a piece of steak.

She has no time to stop and give way.
Can you hear her coming?
Listen to my appealing.
And get out of the way.

Above ground or underground, She
moves at colossal speed.

Some commuters on long distance, Journeys
fall asleep.
Some dive into their story lines.
Some just relax as they view, The
colourful countryside.

Some commuters are excited,
About travelling long distances, To
work, or even to France, By the
snake like machine. She will take you
to your destination, Before you
realise.

# WORK

From creation man had a duty to labour.
Very few are born with gold spoons, In
their mouths.
Using hands and brains for hours and hours.
Work can begin even before age five.
Some individuals plod on well beyond age seventy five.

Work is that task, which before us is set, Or
the task which ourselves we set.
From work comes satisfaction and wages.
In some cases it creates fame and wealth.

Work is not always a bed of roses.
In the process there may be sweat and tears.
Yet the workaholics will not strike, nor fear.
But will strive for their ultimate goals.

Work can help provide social mix and cheer.
Work help provide self esteem.
Work while there is youth and strength.
For the night is coming, when man work no more.

## SAY IT WITH FLOWERS

Sometimes it is I love you.
Sometimes it is I appreciate you.
Sometimes it is I thank you.
Sometimes it is I congratulate you.
Sometimes it is I hope these will cheer you up.
Sometimes it is I want to remember you.
Sometimes it is I want you to remember me.

## THE FASCINATING ROSE

Oh the fascinating rose,
Sheds the most attractive petals, Everywhere
she goes.

The fragrance like unforgettable perfume.
Winged through the air by the gentle winds,
The unforgettable fragrance, Continues
to charm and charm. Even when her
visual presence had gone, From lands
near and far.

Millions have not seen the rose,
Yet this fragrance they treasure and adore.
To create a new rose, bearing her name, Is
a tribute though off by many.

## TRIBUTES TO DIANA

The sea of floral tributes,
That overwhelmed the world, The
various fascinating flowers, Over
chosen grounds.

People travelled from across the globe, Just
to show their concern and love.
Some slept in hotels, Some in sleeping
bags and tents. They gave their respect
and their thoughts, Well deserved.

# RAIN

It poured in torrential showers from high heavens.
Man and beast alike searched for their safe havens.
In caves, in houses, in sheds, in trees, in rock crevices.
Some humans with umbrellas fully propelled.
With clothes saturated and clinging to their frames.

Declining temperature far from usual atmospheric degrees,
Recorded some minutes earlier.
People shiver as wind blow trembling leaves.
Cold rain beat the backs of the bleating goats and sheep.
On the backs of the larger cattle to a lesser degree.

Those indoors delightfully watch the patter of the silver rain drops.
As they land on window panes.
More rain more rest is the opinion of the sluggards.
Busy farmers greet showers of blessing with delight.
The ducks wash their feathers and swim beaming brightly.

# ENDURANCE

Lonely days came.
But with wings they flew. Depression,
an unwelcomed guest, Was not
allowed to take set.
Rescue entered the door on time.

Then the next day was there, Sustaining
strength.
So, she soldiered on amid despair.

Where did her strength come from?
It is God who gave,
Courage and strength.
To plod on; from one day to the next.

Let down by Mr. Adorable.
Tears like rain poured and washed,
Her dainty little face;
Yet always in the limelight.
Despite mistakes.

Was this partly the result,
Of certain traits, In
her character?

# THE BOX THAT SPEAKS

The box shows live pictures, the box that speaks.
Morning noon and night, it never ceases.
Unless switched off. It always has something to offer.
Folks with lots of time on their hands become real fans.

Stories and useful illustrations are shown.
Many children take interest and will learn.
Busy parents pick educative programs for their children,
Whilst they go bread winning or work in the kitchen.

Many people enjoy the comics and the films.
The sceneries and the faces add awareness to their lives.
Some educative films provide hours of worthwhile interest.
Lonely folks can see faces which seem so close.

Appealing advertisement can be seen.
There are activities on land and sea.
Technology and research give great inspiration. The
activity and intelligence of animal also creates
admiration.

Millions can view films at the same time. There
is less need to go to the theatre, Whether it
rains or shines.
No wonder cinemas are less popular.

# FLOWERS

We cannot help but stop and stare.
At the colourful flowers on hills and planes.
Fascinating petals, displaying works of God's fingers.
Cultivated or uncultivated they create beauty.

Admiring a bouquet or less arranged flowers,
Can lift the spirits of the sick, bringing hope and cheer. The
sweet odour of the scented roses perfume the air.
With lasting fragrance.
 Almost unforgettable.

 Flowers play a decorative part in churches. They
add beauty and serenity.
Amid the pianos, organs, elegant paintings, Flowers
stand out and create a welcome effect.

In the homes and work places, flowers are arranged, To
give some obvious and important touches.
Flowers are a popular gift from many wooing males.
Some husbands too present flowers to their spouses.

# THE MARKET POLICE

Men given charge, to exercise their authority,
Their uniform, Blue Navy. Patrolling areas
where traders, Display their products.

Despite being aware, they should,
Not, obstruct the gang way, With
the items they have for sale.
Traders sometimes go against the rules.

On the sight of men in blue navy,
Traders are often being alerted. By
their fellow traders. That the
Market police are on their way.
Immediately, the gangway will be cleared.

At times there is animosity.
Towards the men in blue navy.
As there are complaints, that they,
Dumped items, for people who break the rules. No sympathy shown, that's the traders living, Gone down the drain!

# MOTHER

I am glad that I have a mother so dear.
One who loves and always cares.
The one who taught me to say my first words.
The one who taught me to take my first step.

Mother would not let me cry to disturb the rest.
She provided a shoulder to lean on, before there were no tears left.
She fed me the way she thought to be the best.
When I got tired, she would sing me a lullaby and let me rest.

As a child I got lots of pleasure from objects around me.
Mother instructed me to look without touching.
Not only the pretty things, I was curious about everything. As a little Miss Busybody, I reached the objects, even if it meant climbing.

Mother dear has given me all that she could provide.
My early years she helped to stare and to guide.
Mother believed, in good home training and Christian values.
The discipline she thought, helped me, fit into the wide world.

When I am stressed,
Mother I am sure,
Will help me find solutions.

# FRUITS

Refreshing and tasty.
Stimulating the taste buds.
The starter for the morning meal,
Breakfast time start off with,
Fruit for a source of health, For
each new day.

The exotic fruits, the common fruits,
Pineapple, grapefruit, oranges, tangerine,
Fresh succulent grapes, red or green,
Bananas, mangoes, apples and pears,
So mouth watering. Look! Look!
There is a choice, Take your pick.

Fruits, fruits, they help to give the body stamina.
They suffice the children also the adults.
The soldiers and everyone needs them.
They are a good source of minerals and vitamins.
They assist the bodies' resistance, To certain
maladies.

Fruits are there for the taking at different times of the day.
Preserved, fresh and cooked, Fruit
cakes too are quite delicious.
Made with mixed dried fruits
Including cherries and prunes,
Fermented in wine.

# BIRTHDAY

It is a time of celebration a time of jubilation.
Yet on one's first birthday, one is not aware of the occasion.
Celebration at such a tender age creates a jolly time mainly,
For proud mums and dads, friends and relatives.

It is a time when well wishers send affectionate cards.
Their gifts too show kind thoughts.
A good gathering creates a feeling of well being.

Music is played to liven the atmosphere.
Some guests are stimulated to sing and dance. The
singing of happy birthday, automatically, Brings
smiles to every face.
Then the gentle knocking of wine glasses, Followed
by exciting speeches and laughter.

The adult celebrating their birthday feels a sense of pride. It
is a time of thanks giving.
Thanking God that they have reached, another milestone.
They do not count the cost, as long as they have a jolly time.

The birthday cake is usually nice and enticing.
Most guests look forward to having their slice.
Some alcohol lovers abuse the free drinks and, End
up where they should not be! And awake with
hangovers!

# TRAVEL

Like all living creatures, man need to move about.
In ancient days' travel was mainly by foot.
They also travelled on the backs of animals.
Such as horse, donkey, cows and camels.

Man goes to sea by the use of canoes and boats.
In search of fish and other sea foods.
Man must move in search of food.
Man must move to improve his chance of survival.
Years ago the use of buggies was quite common.

Then buses and coaches were built.
They appear to run at high speed on the broad highway.
They get man about much faster than on foot.
Draining of energy is lessened also ware of the foot.

Man must have envied the birds, which are able, To travel at incredible speed.
Hence the dream of building a machine with wings.
This form of transport has the appearance of a large bird.
When in use it ascends, like the king of the skies.

Some people travel to other lands, in search of work.
Some to collect information, to brink home for their work.
Some for pleasure such as skiing, rock-climbing and sightseeing.
Some travel in search of those special items. To
deck their parlour like "Queen's Palace" Some
travel in search of fame.
With the ambition of getting in the Guinness book of records.

# SIXTY

Once I thought sixty was far, far away.
It seemed as if it would take ages to come my way.
But lo and behold, time has caught up with me!
In fact, it is almost on the door step!

Once I thought folks must be grey headed.
And showed many unwanted wrinkles.
But now I know this was a myth.
Though they are getting on in age.

This is the age where in many cases, Knowledge
gained throughout the years, Reached its peak.
Yet, at this stage, some people are just able, To
do things, that interested them from youth.

This is also a time that many dread.
As they see their working life coming to an end.
They wish they could forever share the funny jokes.
And the work load, with the jolly bunch, at work.

When planned, this time can be a thrilling time.
The vacuum in life, can be filled, with new groups of friends.
Taking up those hobbies which lay dormant for years.
A time to relax and enjoy the fruits, of many years of labour.

# ALARM CLOCK

Round and round you go. You
do not seem to tire.
You must do more miles, In a
day, than any human does.

You seem jealous of my resting.
As while I lay down, you are still slaving.
Sometimes whilst in dreamland,
Enjoying the pleasant scenes,
Which I do not wish to end, But
you decide, it must end.

You kick up a fuss, Alarming, Telling
me I'll miss the bus.
I said I must dream some more. And
not be in a world of hustle, And
bustle any more.

It is too early: let me lay my head,
For half an hour more. I cover you
with my extra blanket, So you
hush for a while.
I dozed off, for a little rest,
Then awoke, to hear you are still a pest!

# DEATH

Death has a time to steal people away.
But no one returns to tell the tale.
It does not ask the question.
Are you ready for deportation?
Some people have a little insight, But
for some it is a sudden plight!

It takes the young.
It takes the middle aged.
It takes the decrepit and old.

Never mind the gold.
Never mind the wealth.
Never mind the health.
Never mind the knowledge.

One day or one night,
We must leave this world.
So let us do the right.
And shun the wrong. So we can
inherit the heavenly home, When our
earthly life is done.

# A TIME

A time to be born,
A time to be educated,
A time to grow up, a time to enjoy adult life

A time to build
A time to break down
A time to plant
A time to reap
A time to invest
A time to lose
A time to buy
A time to sell
A time to agree
A time to disagree
A time to explore the unknown
A time to leave other planets alone
A time to flourish
A time to slow down
A time to shrivel and die

A time for the soul,
To go back to our creator.
And our corpse returns to the ground.
From which man was originally formed.

## PAPA, MAMA

How much you are thought of Papa, Mama.
With off springs of a dozen and two.
You loved one and all.
You did what your resources, would allow.

Papa, Mama, we all loves you both.
Though we spurn the beatings and the discipline.
Why did you seem to enjoy the use of the strap or whip?
Which stung our bottoms like scorpions?
Papa, Mama, but especially Mama.

At times we took our feet in hands,
On seeing Papa coming with the whip.
Foolishly we thought, we had escaped a flogging.
Yet days after just at dawn.
Papa would arrest us, while we were still half asleep.
Unexpectedly, we got that impending flogging, We
thought you had forgotten about, Papa!

It was like a love hate relationship.
We loved you then, we love you still.
Years have rolled on but the beatings, Are
still fresh in our memories.

Though all have now attained adulthood, Those
floggings inflicted,
On our tender frame half a century,
More or less, are still vivid,
As though received, only yesterday!

## GRANDMA'S ROCKING CHAIR

A piece of mahogany, a unique work of art.
Our grandma's rocking chair.
Still in condition more than fair.
From it, four generations, Have
found supreme relaxation.

With a keen sense of organisation. A few
breaks from chores, spent in moderation,
Would always be well earned.
Work is what kept her physically trimmed.
Well beyond four score years and ten.

In that ancient rocking chair.
A harp held in her arms so frail.
Came ripples of melodious tunes.
From our spacious drawing room.
Sounds which elated us morn and noon.

At odd times we sneaked away.
And stole our share of paradise, In
grandma's rocking chair.
Rocking away, we often sang,
Ship ahoy; ship ahoy, what great pleasure.

# GRASS

You will find me here, there and everywhere.
Whether you go north, south, east or west.
I am a great source of food for your cattle.
I may even be used to cover your land.

You can see me mainly green.
I can become yellow or brown.
When I am brown, don't frown.
I can become green again.
After some showers of rain.

I cover your lands.
Give attraction to your lawns. Hopping
along me come many birds, In search
of worms.
Useful I am to manure your crops.

My blades many grow low, covering your land.
You use me to form verges.
When left unattended,
I produce tall blades and even flowers.
Appearing to your eyes, pinkish brown and yellow.
My covering of the land reduces erosion.

# THE PARK

The park how serene, how peaceful.
Away from the huff end the puff.
A place where one can sit and think, then rethink.
While breathing the lasting fragrance of the roses.

The eyes can view the mystic fingers of nature.
The colourful flower beds, arranged in many areas.
The umbrella shaped trees.
The large carpet of grass.
The twittering birds, happily flapping their wings.
Sometimes in flocks, sometimes just the odd one or two.
Some search for insects and scraps of food.
The ducks swimming in the lake as they enjoy the cool.

Young children on see-saw, delighted by the fun.
Some folks running, some just laying in the sun.
Some folks taking picture, filling their cameras.
The park, a place which provides pleasure and relaxation.

## WASHING MACHINE

Clothes and other items can be loaded,
Into its large circular vacuum. By
separating whites from coloureds, A
satisfactory wash can be done.

For some women washing, Used to
be every Monday mornings.
With a mountain of dirty clothing, The
washing tub and scrubbing brush,
Had to be in operation.

The washing machine gives relief, From
the draining of energy.
Though heavy dirt and stains,
Still need bleaching,
Before machine washing.

Perhaps the most tedious task of the week, Used
to be, the weekly hand washing.
Now the machine, will take care of the washing.
Now no need for hands to become water soaked.
Or suffer skin allergy, through soap powder.
Thanks to the washing machine inventor.

# THE ZOO

The zoo is an entertaining exhibition.
It allows children to identify with the natural.
Rather than, pictures and descriptions.
The zebra with necks long and elegant.
Their striped shiny coat, fascinate, The
youths as well as the mature.

The attractive feathers of the various birds.
Are greatly admired, as they hop and flap their wings.
As though their spectators to entertain.
They make unique sounds as if to chatter.
But who can understand bird language?

Many youngsters are fascinated, By
the monkeys antics.
They will share their apples and bananas, So
that the monkeys will not quickly vanish.

Visitors should heed the warning signs,
Shown by the lions' cage, since, They
can be vicious creatures.

The colourful trees, shrubs and flowers, Capture
the attention of all visitors.
Some visitors load their cameras, With
pictures of their memorable day.

# THE BUS

They should be all day busy, busy.
Yet sometimes no bus, no bus. Passengers
must work out the time to be, At work for
their bosses.
They must not be late.
When they are going through the gate.

The buses should run according to schedule.
But some drivers seem to break the rules.

Through late buses some patients miss their medicals.
If they turn up over ten minute late,
They are told, they cannot be treated that day.
New appointment has to be made.

Some school buses are on the road.
Relieving some parents of bearing the load.

Weekend and holidays buses are crammed.
Hardly sufficient space for disabled and prams.

Occasionally passengers have their dogs occupying seats.
I do not think dogs should be allowed on passenger seats!
What says you?

## MICE

Nuisance they are.
They invade from year to year.
They make their way into our houses.
Despite closing doors at dusk.

We do not keep a cat.
But we set mice poison and traps.
Their entry into our house, Is
difficult to stop.

They do not choose, where to go, High
or low.
Sometimes it is on the kitchen work top.
Sometimes it is on the cooker top.
Sometimes it is on the dining table.
Sometimes it is on the floor.
Sometimes it is even in the sofa.

Being small creatures they,
Do not need a lot to get their fill.
They will choose, ripe banana from the fruit bowl.
Bread, cake, or cheese crumbs, on the floor.

The mice poison does work, Once
they devour it instead of food.
Their movements slow down,
Instead of running like lightning.
Their hiding places are usually, Under
the fridge, or under the cooker.
At this stage, they can be found dead,

Ready to be disposed of before decay.

# Funfair

Looking forward to the funfair,
You need to save up for your fare.
And for the exciting entertainment there.
Friends and family invited to go, Even
if they are currently on the dole.

Arrangement made for coach picking up points.
Each passenger need to be at the spot.
Organisers expect you to turn up on the dot.
Early start out in the cool of the day.
As journey could be more than one.
Hundred miles away.

On reaching your destination.
There are a lot of entertainments.
It is sometimes difficult to make, A
decision which first to choose.
The electric swirling cars attract,
Many holiday makers who like such fun.
Up in the air they seemed thrilled.
They enjoyed their hilarious excitement.
Those with height phobia choose less risky pleasures.
There are many games which brings delight.

Ice cream and light refreshments,
Can be purchased whilst enjoying the excitement.

## Spectacles

We can be spectators without spectacles. But
they assist our impaired vision.
When ageing eyes are becoming dim,
They help us to read find prints, Without
eye muscle strains.

With the help of spectacles,
We can read clearly vehicle numbers plates.
Also notices and fine printed books and labels.
We need not ask anyone to read our letters.
The contents of which we do not always, Wish
to share.

Spectacles do not need our hands, To
hold them in place.
Our pair of ears anchors them in place.
It is a good thing we have a pair of ears.
And not just one single ear. Spectacles
are more manageable than,
Magnifying glasses.

## THE BEGGAR

The unkempt looking man.
About middle aged called Herman.
He sits at the same spot daily.
He plays his guitar mainly.
Religious tunes which are quite moving.
Occasionally he says "can I have, Some
money for a cup of tea.
"And a sandwich please?" According
to some individuals, This is his way of
living for some years.

Sympathetic people passing by, drop their,
Coins in a box, which sits,
On the pavement, close to the beggar.

One man passing by tells him, To
go and claim his dole.
Instead of wearing clothes with holes.
Another said, "you scrounger, You scrounger"
The beggar just kept playing and playing, His
entertaining tunes.

# The Almighty

He reigns in heaven as well as on earth.
He sends the rain that we see and hear.
He gives the breath we breathe.
He sends the wind in whatever manner it behaves.
He created the vast ocean so man can sail.
And fish for food.
He allows the golden sun to shine by day.
The Silver Star to shine by night.  He
created the grey and blue clouds,
Which stretches above the earth.
As far as human eye can see.

He gives life which begins in the womb.
After development we pop out into the world.
For how long we do not know!

## Walking stick

It is my aide it supports me.
It is like an arm to lean on.
When I am walking out.
It stops me tripping over.
My walking stick gives me confidence.
It keeps me uphill, it helps me downhill.

Recently I have the pleasure, Of
living in a bungalow.
But I still rely on my walking stick.

I live alone but should,
Anyone burgle my home,
I would whack him, With
my walking stick.

# Birds

Birds, birds how they fly.
They fly low, they fly high.
Way up in the sky.
Man can scarcely reached so high.

Some birds migrate from continent, To
continent.

Outdoors they seem quite content. They
don't look for a tent.
What if they needed to rent a tent?
Who would pay the rent? No one
would consider money to lend, As the
birds could not repay a penny.

Good job they don't need a house.
They don't need a cage,
Only if man choose them to tame.
They will stay in the cage.
But would be happier flying free.
As we can see when they are caught, Then
released, They must say what a relief!

# POLICE

Sometimes in two's, sometimes alone.
Apparent waste of time.
Patrolling the streets, day after day.
Whatever the time, rain or shine.
But must investigate the crime.

By this their glittering foot wear,
Must be wearing thin their soles.
Some resident remarked,"Poor souls".

He must be brave.
She must be brave.
No cowards can face their race.
A task I would not crave.

The bobby on the beat.
Welcomed by some on the street.
Some can't bear their sights.
Fear and anger churn their insides.

No loan bobby should operate; What about his fate?
More measures of safety create, Radio may not save his heart or face.

# THE SEA

A large body of salty water.
People will always sort after it. They
need what it has to offer.
The fishermen must sail.
Out in the deep.
To set their fishnets. They
have to make a living,
From their drafts.

At times the sea can be boisterous.
It can be heard roaring, Like
vicious lions. At such times the
fishermen, Have to abandon their
nets.
After the storm there will be calm.
So fishermen are safe to bring in their haul.

Visitors can relax on the shore.
As they enjoy the refreshing sea breezes.
Some go swimming for the soaking and exercise.
Some collect sea shells to take home.
Some get their fill of fresh fish meals.
Right there on the beach.

Occasionally there are accidents at sea.
With ships as well as small vessels.
Rescue operation is carried out.
Most times lives are saved.

# GOD'S CREATION

Behold the beauty of the world.
The firmament wide spread. The
majestic moon.
The shining stars, Giving
light by night. The sun with
glittering rays, To light the
world by day.

The mountains decked, With
various shrubs and trees.
Rocks shaped as if,
Human hands have carved!
Yet they have no part, In
such work of art.

The seas and the rivers.
Are there for man to sail and fish.
The attractive sandy beaches,
With sea stones and sea shells, For
man's use and pleasure.
The birds flying low and soaring high.
Their humming and beauty to admire.
The grass for the cattle.
There is a purpose for everything.

## FEET

Thank heavens for my durable feet.
As I grew they got bigger and stronger.
My feet help me to tread this lovely earth.
They take me here there and everywhere.
Places where cars, buses and trains cannot take me.

They take me up hill among pebbles.
Among narrow tracks, and rock climbing.
My feet help me to walk, run and jump.
They do not go on strike.

What if I had no feet?
I'd have to rely on crutches.
Or get around in special chair.
My feet are made to last my life time.

# THE SUN

You show your glittering face.
Beneath the morning skies.
Soliciting its time to rise and shine.
As the day goes on you spread, Your
welcoming rays.

At dawn you glitter on the due.
You later clear the mist.
Man's heart you warm with elated spirit.
As body temperature rises,
They automatically obtain more energy.

Young kids and lambs skip and feed at their leisure.
Cows graze and feed in pastures at their pleasure.
Birds sing as they flap their wings. Insects march
out of their dens, In search of food for breakfast.

At eve you disappear behind the clouds.
Reaching brethren on the other, Side of
the world.

# LOVE

A devoted attachment,
Which does not alter. Despite
the odds,
It's an everlasting tie. Which
remains forever and forever It will
endure upheavals.
But will remain unchanged.
It will endure the test.
Even though it may cause upset.
It holds out even in gloom.
It stands unchanged.
Uphill,
Downhill, Or in
the valley.

## LOOKING BACK

I see disappear, I see hope.
I see sadness, I see joy.
I see tears, I see laughter.
I see fears, I see confidence.
I see disappointment, I see achievement.
I see death, I see births.
I see sickness, I see healing.
I see weathering, I see growth.
I see poverty, I see wealth.
I see decay, I see building up.
I see hate, I see love.
I see dislike, I see friendship.
I see war, I see peace.

# TEARS

The fluid which can be seen,
Running down from the eyes then down the cheeks.
Tears may be considered a language.
It may be translated as:
The expression of inward sorrow.
The expression of inward joy.

Some people when unsuccessful,
Shed tears sorrowful. Some
people when successful, Shed
tears joyful.

The shedding of tears, Can help to
relieve stress. Yet too much tears,
when grieving, Can lead to ill
effect.

A daughter I know,
Shed tears, and tears, and tears.
Perhaps enough a rat to drown!
She cried until, weeks after her mum was put down.

I offered comfort.
Hoping her blood pressure would go down; In
order that she would not drop down.

# LANGUAGE

Throughout the universe, Man
must express himself.
Language is the key. Revolving
around his thoughts, His
emotions and his want.

He uses language to command.
He uses language to demand.
He uses language to reprimand.

He uses language for merchandise.
He uses language in writing As
well as verbally.

Through language man, Can
learn.
Can laugh.
Can cry.
Can sigh.
Can sing.

## MOTOR CAR

Oh what a wonderful thing you are.
Motor car, motor car.
You give me great pleasure.
Especially when cruising, Along
country lanes at leisure.

All year round.
In the rain, the wind, the snow, and the cold.
You give me the needed guard.
Though when it's summer, You
get as hot as an oven.

You are really handy.
You are my little Pandy.
Without you, how would I manage the shopping?
Especially on days when I am hopping.

The pessimist kept saying, Where
will you find the financing?
For insurance and the road tax.
Let alone the many litres of petrol.
And to get you repaired.

I reflect on the saying,
Where there is a will, There
is a way!
I'll give priority to my little motor.

# MUSIC

We are told that, there is music in heaven.
Earth too needs its share.
To lighten each burden.
To uplift the mood during worship.
To create a happy atmosphere during work.

It is like medicine to the weary.
It lifts the spirit of the weak.
It is appreciated by every nation.
It is sorted more, by each generation.

Let gloom and sorrow take their flight.
Let joyous sounds disperse the sad plight.
Play on, play on, sounds so soothing.
Play on, play on, sounds so moving.

Let the jolly move with elation.
Others too will catch on.
Thrilling and filling their whole being.
Play on; play on, from morn till night.

During the swinging parties and concerts, The young as well as elders move with magic waves.
Play on, play on, and let the happy moments roll!

## Soil

Here I have been years upon years.
Long before you were ever born.
Humans come and humans go.
But I live to tell the tale.
Your existence depends largely upon me.
The crops I nourish provide you with food.
Deep, deep down you find water.
On my surface water Too-Lakes rivers and seas.

You anchor huts, mansions and skyscrapers upon me.
So much you obtain from me.
Diamonds, silver, gold and aluminium.

Simple and sophisticated tools you use to till me.
Such tedious toils I admire, then smiling said I.
"Toil on, toil on, till toiling days are done".
For some anxiety runs high,
About taking their flight in winter.
What 'ere the climb, you'll be fine.
Fear not little ones you are part of me.
Toil on, toil on, and toil on.
One day, toiling you will complete.
Your souls will with our master be.
Then you will come to be with me forever.

# Alone

One can enjoy one company, Without being insane.
Away from the crowded places.
One can turn back the pages.
And look down life's stages.

Where there have been mistakes.
One can look back, and then say.
I will not fall, into that ditch again.

Occasionally as a youngster I spent, An hour or two in the Kentish graveyard,
Relaxing with a book.
Or just strolling along the footpath.
I admired the beautiful flowers.
And the greenery around.
There was rarely anyone around.
Away from the gardener.
Or just hummingbirds.
I saw no ghost among the tombs!
I always enjoyed,
The fresh air in the tranquillity.

# The cruise

It was a sunny afternoon, shortly after lunch.
Together we were as a friendly bunch.
We sat relaxed on benches near the flowerbeds.
Which were quite close to the river base.
The sun streaming brightly upon us.
The cruise boat making voyages.
Passengers boarding with smiles.
We decided we too must go cruising.
We boarded the next boat available.
As we journeyed along the river, We
took many breaths of fresh air.
Our stresses gradually disappeared,
As we joked and watched the rippling waters. One passenger said "I hope this is not a titanic ship experience".
Another said "this cruise is safety guaranteed". More jokes and laughter followed.
As the journey continued we noticed,
Individuals paddling their own canoes.
All appeared to be having a jolly time.
Our boat continued the mapped out journey.
We all returned to base as happy as larks.

## The willow tree

There she stands with widespread branches.
Its pinnacle seem to be reaching for the sky.
Countless times she hears the church bell.
She must be getting old.
My granddad said "she has been always green.
Ever since he and Nan were children".
Her lower branches can be seen bowing.
Always appear full of the joys of spring.

She has shaded passing children.
And adults too, from the scorching sun.
And sheltered many from the rain.
She provides the welcome base.
For the birds to roost and nest.
A safe heaven,
For the young to hatch and thrive.
She has seen many passers-by, Some
gossiping, some giggling, Some sad,
some glad.
Some watched her numerous leaves dancing.
And at times in the wind her branches whistling.

## The beef scare

Dazed and weak they seemed.
Minutes later legs collapsed.
Bodies slumped to the ground.
Unpleasant! But the plight diagnosed.

Though rare, the disease is transferable to man.
An air of fear is instilled within the mind.
In ninety-five we were told, Ten
cases diagnosed, one deceased.

Hence slaughtering of certain cattle.
Poor creatures! Poor creatures!
Better though than carrying the guilt, Of
any further loss of man's life, Through
consuming the beef.

Actions taken, corrective steps, To
make beef safe.
A curious customer, asked about sales,
Butcher Smith replied hesitantly, "Sales
remain much the same" A few weeks
later the situation changed. From the
once jubilant Butcher Smith, One could
hear a sigh.

With the burden hard to bear, Some
farmers have given up in despair.
One committed suicide, quit forever!
Some are sad yet want to stage the fight.
"My livestock, my livestock"

Cried Farmer Woodstock with little optimism, The government would compensate.

# WHAT AM I?

What am I?
Succulent I am
Clusters I am on the vine
Green and red
Pick me
Eat me fresh
Juice me
Turn me
Into wine
Drink me
When you
Want to
Wine and dine  What
am I?

# Can you guess?

Very juicy am I.
Stimulate your taste buds.
I am liked by you, as well as girls and boys.
A source of vitamins for your body.
You many have me as a starter breakfast.
I am more refreshing later, When the sun is blazing.
Even better with a few ice cubes.
You can eat me fresh.
Just pick me from the tree at harvest. You may wish to juice and bottle me. Some preserving will make me last, Months after harvest.
What am I?

## Hygiene

Nowhere is entirely germs free.
Germs are so tiny we need, The
microscope to see them. It is
worth protecting ourselves,
From the illnesses they cause.

Adhering to good hygiene, Will
pay off.
Hand washing after wee or poo.
Ensuring to use of water and soap.
Avoid dirty hands touching surfaces and foods.

Foods must be covered.
As flies seem to enjoy what we prepare, For
ourselves and not for them.
Flies do not only steal our meals, But
leave on them their germs, Which
we will ingest.

Habitually disinfecting washbasins,
Baths, drains and bins, Will
keep germs at bay.

## My kitchen

Here the daily preparation is done for food.  In
order to sustain life we have to cook.
Eggs and bacon with tomatoes and onions,
For breakfast quite appetising I find,
For lunch one of our favourite dishes,
Is fish and chips,
With green peas,  And fresh
salad with beetroot.
Then mixed fruit juice, to follow.

My older daughter likes to mix,
The ingredients for the cake,
Also the dough to cut,
For the meat patties and apple pies.

I told Molly, we must cover all foods.
To prevent those big flies,  Perching
upon our foods.
They could be carrying dangerous germs.

It takes almost as much time cleaning up,
As preparing and doing the cooking.  My
husband does some washing up,  But
with a face frowning.

# Jermaine

The boy only seven.
But it looks like eleven.
They call him Jermaine.
But what is his surname?

He is tall and thin.
Smooth as velvet his skin.
He is as quiet as a lamb.
Find his match, not in this land.

He has keen interest.
In the music he plays,
Some mystical tunes, They
are always thrilling.

His appetite is fairly good.
He does not like tin foods. He
likes to tuck into mom's,
Home cooking foods. He also
likes bread-and-butter, With
loads of peanut butter.
Salad dish and fresh fruits, are never too much.

# Evening

A time when the golden sun goes down.
Hiding its face behind the running clouds. A
time when the scorching heat subsides.
Giving a change to temperate moderate.
The gentle winds have branches and leaves swaying.

Many lovers' take their timely strolls.
As each other's hands they hold.
Enjoying the breezy air so cool.
Some are seeing just relaxing on lawns.
Some get carried away with TV programs.
Or their favourite books.

For some it is a time to reflect, After
the day's events.
Was everything done as meant?
For some folks evening is a time,
To go out to meet friends and for entertainment, Be
they church, pubs, clubs or parties.

For other folks evening is the time, To
relax body and mind.
After the days hustle and bustle.
No one should interrupt or be a pest.

## I am scared of the dark

"I am scared of the dark" Said
little Anny.
"Can you put the lights on Peggy?" She
begged.
"Without the lights on "
"I will not go to the loo," "I am scared
of the bogeyman". Peggy replied, "I
will put the lights on" "No need to be
scared".
They once shared the same bedroom.
But as little Annie's, loud snores,
Kept Peggy awake. Peggy moved
Into the spare bedroom. When
little Anny got back to bed,
Peggy sang her a lullaby.
Then said, "night night, pleasant dreams".

## Market

With times so hard.
And finances so low.
I have to watch my budget.
So I have got to find the bargains.

Cut price, cut price especially on evenings.
Traders want to get rid of stock.
On Saturday late afternoon, I was in shocked.
Half price, for all vegetables per box, Eggs,
meat, fish and fruit were also half price.

With children soon to go to college,
I have to gradually save the pennies.
So even for kitchen utensils, And for
shoes and clothes. I find the
markets instead, Of the
supermarket.

At the end of the year I check my savings.
When compared with supermarket, I
was pleasantly surprised.
As I have managed to save a decent sum.

# Money

"Money can't buy health".
There is grain of truth in this saying,
Since if disease is incurable,
The millionaire will not be cured,
Even though he has he spent most of his saving.

We cannot fly like the birds.
We must pay for travel even on the buses.
We must pay for the roof over our heads.
Be it rent or be it mortgages.

Money is needed to purchase food.
Food is the staff of life. If
we go on a hunger strike,
For more than two weeks.
We will surely die.

Without financial problems in the way,
Children should be able to concentrate and study,
Money is needed for the education, So
that they can reach their potential.

Every now and then we hear of people, Risking
their lives, leaving their country.
For a better life, in another country. But
some don't make it, they get drowned,
What a sad situation!

## Handsworth Park

School children lining, The
large lake.
Admiring the ducks and ducklings.
The educator guarding, The kids
like a hawk.
Making sure that none depart.

Ducks swimming in the deep,
Beaks down, then up again,
Whilst picking at the undergrowth, Obtaining
some nutrients.
Later with flapping wings, They
reached the edge of the lake.

The duck search the surrounding grounds. Finding
foods for lunch.
Scraps of meat and bread, Bits of
apple, green and red. Strolling kids
and adults bring them, Food that
they may feed.

The sweet fragrance of the roses blooming.
Picked up in the breathing.
Whilst the gentle breeze is blowing.
Trees full of the joys of spring. Providing,
cooling, cooling for the pores, At noon
when the hot sun bakes.
Some folks seen walking for exercise.
Some just relaxing on the benches,
Whilst others laze on the green grass, All welcome the ice
cream van, when it comes hooting, ready for cooling.

## Supermarkets

Many supermarkets have sprung up.
Knocking out the smaller traders wherever they go.
Whilst the giants supermarkets are blooming.
The small businesses are losing.
In fact they are dwindling fast.

Some supermarkets have extra shelves.
Having items stocked to their tops,
Nearly every item can be found, Under
one cover.

Opening hours twenty four seven, Is
becoming the norm.
Some working customers find it convenient.
Businesses that used to be closed by seven,
Are now open much later,
Even on Sundays
Why so many hours?
Has the world gone crazy?
Or is it just greed?

# Trees

In autumn some trees shed their leaves,
Come winter they stand apparently dead!
Then in spring they begin to leaf and bud,
But thanks be to the Evergreen,
All year round some greenery can be seen
Some trees grow mighty high, As though
to touch the sky!
The umbrella shaped trees provide shade,
From the blazing sun rays, And shelter
when it rains.

Some trees have lifespan longer than mans',
Providing fruit for up to four generations,
Some birds build their nest in the trees,
Where they lay eggs have the young thrive,

Some trees grow roots long, long, Anchoring
them firmly in the soil.
And guarding them against, Erosion
when there is a storm.

Trees are also useful when hewed,
Despite the increased use of glass and metal. Trees
will always be in demand for furniture and ships,
Trees were from creation.

## Memorable Holiday

From Brum to Bronx.
My brother and sister sponsored.
I did not hesitate,
To accept the offer to the states.

Even before the date,
I was so elated,
I started to relate, To
friends and family.
That I was about, To
turn another page.

On the appointed date,
I left Brum,
For seven hours flight to Bronx.
At Bronx airport we met. On
reaching my sister's home,
Another exciting time.

We chatted over the appetising meal,
Until the early hours of morn. Time
for my brother to say bye, bye, Until
next day after his work.

The following week I spent quality time, With
my brother and his family.
Then four days were spent in Canada.
We attended our nephew's wedding. And
visited Niagara Falls.
To put the icing on the cake,

I spent eight days with my niece in Texas. I had a great time.

## Christmas

A time for Christ's birth to be celebrated.
A time when family and friends meet.
A time to have some extra feast.
A time for gifts to be exchange.

At Christmas, decorations of various colours, Are
arranged in homes, businesses and towns.
Children go door-to-door singing.
With merry voices thrilling.
Away in a manger no crib for a bed.
The little Lord Jesus, lay down his sweet head.
Charitable folks give them cash, To boost
their Christmas gifts. They show their
appreciation by saying, "Thank you".

Father Christmas brings stockings, Full
of goodies.
Just what he knows the children need.
Some children ask their parents weeks before,
"Mum, dad, what are we having for Christmas?"
The extra food and drinks,
Are there to enjoy, but everyone,
Should avoid, getting drunk, Over
the Christmas season.

## Storm

Prediction by the astrology, Indicated
residents should be, Prepared to
evacuate.
Farmers to bring in their herds and not hesitate.

It happened on the dot.
And at the expected spot.
The boisterous winds activated on the date.
Ripping the tree branches, throwing roof slates.
In a number of cases there was not one left.

Torrential showers caused flooding. Sheep
uncared for all bleating.
Men, women and children running.
Those who slighted the warning, Refer
to what happened as devastating.

Residents who did not seek any early
shelter, Had to be lifted by a helicopter.
Before further devastation or loss of life.

Overcrowded hurricane centres and schools, Provided
hot food.
Yet the flashing lightning and clamours, Of
thunder have residents inside churned.

The continuous heavy downpour, Left
fields swamped.
The crops washed away, soil drenched.
Building gutted, what a nightmare!

## Feeling inferior

Fearful to face the crowd,
Even if offered several pounds.
No desire to go upfront.
Will take the back seat for comfort.
Rayon many times refused invitations,
To attend entertainments.
Prefers to remain in his four walls.
To prevent sweat glands overworking.
Heart beating thump, thump, thump.

Even actors have fears,
When appearing on stage, For
their first performance.

Mark's brother Rayon,
Had preferred being isolated,
Until Mark related, That all
humans are equal. So He
should not be afraid, Of
people's faces. Then Mark
assured his brother, That he
would sit with him.
Through the oncoming rally.
From then his shyness and fears,
Gradually disappeared.

## Sleep

A space to escape,
From consciousness into unconsciousness.
Total relaxation of mind and body.

The best remedy for tiredness, is sleep.
Coffee and tea only gives temporary release.
Some folks have wakeful intervals. There are
those who sleep soundly, As their heads hit
their pillows.
Some sleep so soundly that,
If their houses were on fire,  They
would not even hear the siren!

Mother's voice I heard calling.
This particular morning, I was
still half asleep.
She calls "May, May".
"Get up, get up, you sleepyhead".

She said,
"It'll soon be time for school".
I got up so hurriedly, I nearly fell over the stool.
Got ready in minutes despite my fast gait, I got
to school 15 minutes late.

I had to apologise to Miss Adelate.
 I told her I had overslept.
She warned, "if it occurred again"
"On that evening I would be detained".

## The Human pump

Constantly at work,
As long as we are alive.
Beating about 70 times per minute.
Supplying oxygen to our tissues.  Bump,
bump, bump and so it continues,  Even
during hours of unconsciousness.
We are not always aware,  That
our hearts are at work.
If our hearts stop working,
For many minutes,
Without resuscitation, we would,  Become
corpse!

## House

A place to shelter.
A place to escape.
A place to rest.
A place to sleep.
A place to be alone.
A place to call our own.

People are housed in buildings.
Some made of bricks and slates.
Some made of concrete and stones.
Some made of mortar and stones.
Some made of wood and thatch.
When Mark started to work,
He said, "I must get a house of my own".
He did not only save twenty five percent of his wages,
But every pound he could. After ten years he had a house,  Over his head!

## Rainy day

Molly was quite composed on the sofa.
With eyes grounded in her favourite book.
She heard the patter, on the roof, Almost
as loud as galloping hooves.

While Molly remained wrapped up in her story lines.
The patter, patter, got louder and louder.
Having no special reason to go out, More
rain, more rest, she thought.

Her mother arrived home, soaked to the bone.
Her mother said, "In the sky hung a rainbow"
"Then it was as if the heavens opened," "People
and animals alike ran for shelter".

Molly said, "Mother may I take your coat and hat?"
"You are looking like a drowned rat!"
"How about a cup of your favourite tea?" "Tapped
up with a few drops of brandy".

"Oh! How thoughtful! That will certainly warm me up".
"I'll dry off by the fire, while I await that cupper".
In minutes, Molly handed her mother, A
steaming cup of tea.
"This is wonderful", Says Molly's mother as she sipped.

# Charity

The Good Samaritan did not leave,
The wounded to bleed, Until
there was no blood left. He
took him to an Inn, And paid
for his care.

There are good Samaritans around.
But there is need for many more.
How wonderful it would be,
If all the rich and able, Involved
charity in their plans.

No one in this position, Should
shut bowels of compassion.
Nor allow the sentence to be passed,
I was hungry and you did not feed me!
I was naked and you did not cloth me!

We should be our brothers' keeper.
Seeking out their welfare,
Giving with love, Giving
with willing minds.

## Rubbish

"Tomorrow is Tuesday", says Miss Muggings.
The council garbage truck will be coming, Bag up all your household waste.
All your bottles and cans,
Wash for the recycle bin, put separate.


For unwanted furniture,
Fridges, cooker just call the second hand dealer.
They will give you a few pounds, Which you can give to charity.

Sometimes people come to doors,
Begging a pound,
Give them a helping hand,
With the few pounds from the dealer.

It looks rather untidy,
To see old beds, sofas and other items, Broken up and stacked on the drive.
Better taken to the tip,
Or order a skip,
Keep the surroundings tidy.

## West Indian carnival

It's time again for the annual, West
Indian summer carnival.
Since August 1969, performers prepare, For
the exciting time, this draws a large crowd.

The circus begin on the road.
Performers dressed in eye catching costumes.
Some curious supporters line the roads.
In the park, the circus flows the more.
Children and adults imitate the dance.

A variety of foods and drinks on sale. Supporters
can choose from the many stalls, While enjoying
the music and the fun.

The music and performance, Put
a smile on every face.
Followed by much laughter, Even
if you were sad before.

The excitement continue until dusk.
Supporters wish the fun would never end.

## The squirrel

Exactly where he lives, I do not know.
But every day, he appears rain or snow.
Up and down the garden he runs.
Sometimes he wags his bushy tail.
Exactly where he lives, I do not know!

I know he is scared, of the neighbour's cat.
When the cat comes on the scene.
The squirrel lost his privileges.
And disappeared like a ghost.

He is no more a stranger.
He is almost like a friend.
He enjoys scraps of bread.
Also lean bacon and the rind. He
enjoys apples too.
Sometimes he is seen,
Biting into the fruit, Succulent
and enticing.

Some days, as I curiously gaze.
I see the little creature,
Sitting on the apple tree.
With an apple held secure,
Between his front legs. There
he happily chews away, At his
own leisure.

## Time

As certain incident occur, They
mark milestones in time.
Christ came on earth, Over
two thousand years ago.

Time cannot be seen.
Time is measured by the clock.
And by the watch. By these
measures we can tell, The
time of the day or night.

We were not aware of the time, We
were born.
But we can refer to it, by the record, That
was made at our birth.

In history, times are recorded Of
important incidents.
The time of world war one.
The time of world war two.
The time when Saddam was overthrown.

Very few can tell the time, Their
life will end.
The politician set time, For
the forthcoming election.
But they cannot set a time.
When their life will end, Only God knows.

## Island in the sun

So tranquil were the whispering winds.
Many bamboo, palms and coconut tree,
Waved at us as the gentle winds,
Mobilise their branches and feather like leaves.

Oh, the fascinating deep blue sea,
The beaches of colourful stones and seashells.
A carpet of silvery sand seen.
As far as human eyes can behold.

Energetic children riding their humble ponies,
Some rather tiny yet busy with buckets and spades,
They build mountains; they build houses with sand, Adults
of all nations enjoy pleasuring entertainments.

Temperature soaring despite the gentle sea breeze.
Refreshing fruit punches were selling fast.
The ice cream lavished with nourishment.
And enticing flavour caused many mouths to water.

The smell of mellow fruits,
From grape vineyards, apples and mango groves, Wisp
through the air for miles away.
On our guided tour, we were given lovely grape samples,
Many holiday makers swimming with excitement.
Some offering to share their sun beach rugs, and sun chairs,
Many topless men, women and children, All enjoying the
sun.

## A to Z

A is for apple, one a day keeps the doctor away.
B is for blossom, and then the fruits will follow.
C is for character, be a good fellow.
D id for doctor, take your prescribed dose.
E is for excellent, strive to excel.
F is for feather, birds of a feather flock together.
G is for gold, go for the gold medal.
H is for high, strive for the high marks.
I is for Iris, she is not Irish.
J is for jam, be patient in the traffic jam.
K is for kettle, Polly put the kettle on.
L is for lock, be sure to lock your car door.
M is for majority, one bad apple will spoil the lot.
N is for noun, are you well known? O is for organ, can you play music?
P is for promise, try to keep it.
Q is for quiet, he is as quiet as a lamb.
R is for rest, find time to rest after labour.
S is for safety, be careful not to fall.
T is for together, divided we will fall.
U is for urgent, so don't delay.
V is for victory, don't accept defeat.
W is for war, but I am not for it.
X is for x-ray, it could help save your life, don't run away.
Y is for year, It is speeding away.
Z is for zebra, animals are much admired.

# Dreams

Dreams at times, take over our thoughts during sleep.
People, places and things are seen.
Sometimes voices can also be heard.
Sometimes the incidents are false.
Sometimes the incident happens as seen, In
our dreams.

Years ago I dreamt,
I fell into a pit.
I was very distressed.
But greatly relieved,
When I suddenly awoke,
To find it's false,
I was in dreamland!

On other occasions I dreamt, I
heard my mother calling.
"May, May, it's time to rise and shine."
I looked at the clock,
It was just the right time, For
me to rise for work.

Some dreams are pleasant.
Some dreams foretell,
What's in the future. Some
dreams could do, With an
interpreter.

## Slow Love

Noon was quickly slipping away.
The educators completed the tedious and rewarding task,
The youngsters set out on their homeward track.
There were no trams, no cars, no buses and no trains. No transport to minimise travel after brain searching lessons,
Not even a bicycle.

May's gait was pretty fast.
On her daily journey past, The
home of her aunt Daisy.
She bumped into Dave.
He began talking and laughing.
Then counting down the homeward steps, Out popped the short sentence "I love you!" May was unsure how to respond.
But some interest began.

May started secondary school, Shortly
after they first met.
When she didn't get a bus, He
accompanied her, to her abode,
Again they would meet weekends.

On finishing school shortly after,
May worked away for some months,
Her parents planned her immigration,
To May's surprise, Dave and two acquaintances,
Were on the same flight,
Their friendship continued, Followed by engagement.
Marriage, one year after.

www.ingramcontent.com/pod-product-compliance
Lightning Source LLC
Chambersburg PA
CBHW070625300426
44113CB00010B/1655